MORAY

A pictorial souvenir

NESS PUBLISHING

2   A panoramic view of Lossiemouth beach and the River Lossie estuary.

MORAY

Along Speyside to the sea, and more . . .

Welcome to Moray! Part one: from mountain to sea

The modern-day county of Moray encompasses as wide a variety of scenery and depth of history as any part of Scotland. The boundary changes of 1974 saw it absorb the southern part of neighbouring Banffshire and this greatly expanded the 'new' county's geographical range. Thanks to this re-organisation, the south-western boundary of Moray passes through the summits of Cairn Gorm and Ben Macdui (second highest mountain in Britain). From this 1220m/4000ft plateau, Moray sweeps down Strath Avon and Glen Livet to glorious Speyside, world-renowned for its salmon fishing and malt whisky.

Moray also lost some territory to the same boundary changes, its former south-western corner being taken into the Highland Region. This included the town of Grantown-on-Spey, so in acknowledgement of its recent past and to allow inclusion of more of Speyside, this book will stretch a point and visit that area too. It should also be said that the Banffshire name has not been extinguished, with many people and businesses on Speyside retaining the old county's name in their addresses.

As the county unfolds from the mountains to the sea, it embraces rich farmland that produces an abundance of crops, including the top-quality barley needed by the distilleries. Other crops include wheat, oilseed rape, potatoes and other vegetables. Dairy and beef farming are strong while sheep farming remains despite difficulties in that sector. And these days farming of an entirely different type is visible on the Moray hills in the form of wind turbines.

Moray begins here! The county's western boundary runs through the summits 5
of Cairn Gorm and Ben Macdui, forming an arc around chilly Loch Avon.

The richness of the land has meant that Moray has been home to humankind for at least four millennia. The Picts ('painted people') have left dramatic evidence of their occupancy of the region: one of the most magnificent Pictish standing stones in Europe has been re-erected in Forres. Standing over 6m/20ft tall, Sueno's Stone was unearthed in 1726 and is estimated to have been carved in the 9th or 10th century. The name 'Moray' can be traced back to the 10th or 11th century, when it related to a much larger region ruled by a Gaelic-speaking dynasty, the best-known member of which was the infamous Macbeth, king of Scots from 1040 to 1057.

Elgin is the county town of Moray and location of many places of interest that reflect its long history. King David I (r. 1124-1153) granted Elgin royal burgh status; in 1224 it became the seat of the Bishop of Moray. The Cathedral, although a ruin, is one of the finest examples of medieval architecture in Scotland. Castle remnants can still be seen on Lady Hill and the town centre boasts a fine array of houses that reflect the styles of successive eras.

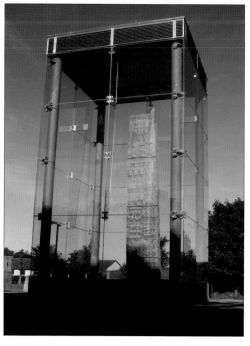

Sueno's Stone.

The varied canvas of Moray is completed by its coastal strip that offers a rich variety of towns and villages. Most of these have their origins in the fishing industry, which is still active in some of them. Lossiemouth's magnificent beaches are a match for any seaside rival and so extensive that they are never crowded. The Moray Firth micro-climate extends its benevolent influence to this part of the coast and the waters of the firth are home to dolphins, seals and many species of seabirds.

So, for residents and visitors alike, Moray provides something for everyone. Whether it is your home or your destination, the aim of this book is give a taste of that variety and so encourage exploration, from mountain tops to seaside rocks – happy venturing!

Ornamental drinking fountain 7
in the village of Tomintoul.

8   Founded in 1824 by George Smith, The Glenlivet Distillery is the home of one of the world's most famous malt whisky brands and is open to visitors for tours and tastings.

It is one of eight distilleries that form the Malt Whisky Trail, the other members of which will be indicated by (MWT) where they appear in this book.

10 The village of Tomintoul, on the edge of the Glenlivet Crown Estate and in the Cairngorms foothills, is the highest village in the Highlands at around 355m/1160ft.

Further down Glen Livet by the B9008 is the Old Bridge of Livet. **11**
As built, it spanned the river in three arches, one of which was washed away in the floods of 1829.

12 Attractively laid out Grantown-on-Spey, built to the plan of Sir James Grant, used to be in Moray and is the westernmost point in this book. This is the north end of The Square.

The Revack Estate is just outside Grantown. Set in 350 acres of outstanding scenery with a walled garden, **13** ornamental lochans and trails to explore, this picture captures the woodland beauty of the estate.

14 Ballindalloch is one of the most beautiful and renowned castles in Scotland. Known as the Pearl of the North, it is located in the heart of Speyside, near to many famous whisky distilleries.

A much loved family home, Ballindalloch is one of the few privately owned castles to have been lived in continuously by its original family. The Macpherson-Grants have resided there since 1546. **15**

16 The old Bridge of Avon, across the road from Ballindalloch Post Office.

The former railway viaduct at Ballindalloch now forms part of the Speyside Way.

The Speyside Way long-distance walk stretches 65 miles from Aviemore to Buckie on the Moray coast   **17**
(see p.72). It uses sections of the former Speyside railway, as here at Tamdhu (formerly Knockando) station.

18 Cardhu Distillery (MWT) at Knockando was established officially in 1824.

Across the Spey to the south, a retired still provides a point of interest at Glenfarclas Distillery.

Glenfarclas (meaning 'Valley of the green grass' in Gaelic) Distillery has the largest stills on Speyside. **19**
This is its Visitor Centre.

20 Outside of the Cairngorms, Ben Rinnes is the highest hill in Moray at 840m/2755ft.
The inset picture is a close-up of the granite outcrops visible in the main view.

Continuing eastwards, and back on the northern bank of the Spey, we come to the
pleasing village of Archiestown. In 2010 it will be celebrating its 250 year anniversary.

22 The Spey between Aberlour and Craigellachie, a view which sums up Speyside: the river wrapped in the wooded hills with arable and livestock farming on its banks.

An autumn scene looking north-east across the village of **23**
Charlestown of Aberlour with Ben Aigan (471m/1540ft) in the distance.

24 Turn the book through 90° to appreciate this aerial view of the River Spey as it passes Aberlour. It shows the neat plan to which the village was built.

The group of large buildings is the H.Q. of Walkers, the famous shortbread manufacturer. **25**
The picture on p.22 is looking along this stretch of the river from top to bottom.

26 Aberlour Church of Scotland kirk. The settlement grew on the site of the church and well dedicated to Saint Drostan, and was developed in 1812 by Charles Grant of Wester Elchies.

Along with the eight distilleries, the Speyside Cooperage (just outside the village of Craigellachie on the Dufftown road) is the ninth venue on the Malt Whisky Trail.

28 A few miles further along Speyside is the village of Rothes, home of the Glen Grant Distillery (MWT), seen here from the slopes of Ben Aigan across the valley.

The Glen Grant Distillery (MWT) in Rothes is noted **29** for its fine garden as well as its excellent whisky.

30 Exterior and interior views of Baxter's Museum Shop in Fochabers, a Speyside village north of Rothes.

This leaping salmon sculpture greets visitors to Fochabers as they enter the village from the east. **31**
The Spey is one of Scotland's greatest salmon fishing rivers.

32 And finally the River Spey flows into the sea here at Spey Bay, 98 miles from its source in the Monadhliath Mountains. Inset: a fine sculpture of an osprey at Spey Bay.

The Spey flows into the outer Moray Firth, well known for its Bottlenose Dolphins. **33**
The Whale & Dolphin Conservation Society has a visitor centre at Spey Bay.

34 Brodie Castle is near Moray's western border, close to Forres. This fine 16th-century tower house is packed with enough art and antiques to keep connoisseurs happy all day!

The Findhorn river, pictured here at Logie, south of Forres, **35** is rated by some as Scotland's most beautiful river.

36 Logie Steading, in its tranquil, park-like setting, provides visitors with a place for both relaxation and exercise – browse the shops, walk along the Findhorn to Randolph's Leap or enjoy the gardens.

Logie's Longhorn cattle, the breed that originally made
British beef famous, are one of the oldest traditional breeds.

Logie House stands above **37**
the walled garden.

38 Just outside Forres, Dallas Dhu Historic Distillery (MWT) is an industrial museum perfectly maintained in working order. This unique time capsule is in the care of Historic Scotland.

Forres has been a Royal Burgh Town since about 1140. This is Tolbooth Street.

Nelson's Tower was erected in 1806 in celebration of Lord Nelson's victories.

40 From its position on the Cluny Hills above Grant Park, the top of Nelson's Tower gives fine views in all directions, like this one of Findhorn Bay and village to the north of Forres.

The 70ft tower was built by public subscription as a meeting place, viewpoint **41**
and landscape centrepiece and is open to the public on summer afternoons.

42 Forres is well known for its award-winning floral sculptures,
two of which make a magnificent display here in Grant Park.

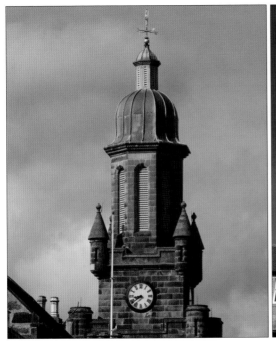

The upper section of Forres Tolbooth, completed in 1849.

The Market Cross, built in 1844, incorporates **43** the base of an earlier, 17th century, cross.

44 St Laurence's Church. Of the many fine buildings in Forres, this is perhaps the most impressive. The interior is worthy of inspection too. Built 1904-1906.

Benromach Distillery (MWT) is located on the northern edge of Forres. Although the smallest **45** working distillery in the Speyside area, it produces 150,000 – 250,000 litres per year.

46 Kinloss Abbey is about two miles north-east of Forres. Founded in 1150 by the Cistercian Order, it became one of the most influential monasteries in Scotland until its demise in 1560.

Another few miles east is Duffus Castle, the original seat of the De Moravia (Moray) family. **47**
One of the finest examples of a 12th-century motte and bailey castle in Scotland.

48 Compared with the picture on pp.40-41, this view gives a very different impression of Findhorn Bay, a popular location for pleasure boating of many kinds.

The former fishing village of Findhorn, four miles from Forres, is nowadays home to the Findhorn **49** Foundation, a thriving holistic community and eco-village. This view is near the village centre.

50 Going east from Findhorn we come to Burghead. This headland was once 'The biggest Iron Age fort in Britain', a Pictish stronghold from the 4th to 7th centuries. Pictured: remaining earthworks.

Burghead harbour still sees a certain amount of fishing activity. **51**
The nearby Visitor Centre has displays that illustrate and interpret the Pictish Fort.

52 A few miles inland is Pluscarden Abbey. Founded in 1230, it is the only medieval monastery in Britain still inhabited by monks and being used for its original purpose. Visitors are welcome.

Glen Moray (MWT) has been distilling single malt whisky since 1897. **53**
On the western outskirts of Elgin, it welcomes visitors for tours and tastings.

54 Elgin town centre boasts many architectural styles, some of which are captured in this picture. On the left, the top of the former Arnott's building looks across to St Giles' Church, right.

These gardens adorn the area at the base of Lady Hill, site of Elgin's castle, some remains of **55** which can still be seen at the top of the hill. The column was erected in 1839 (see over).

56 Close-up of the statue of the fifth Duke of Gordon which stands atop the column on Lady Hill.

Cooper Park, gifted to the town by George Cooper in 1903.

St Giles' Church, built between 1825 and 1828, seen from the **57**
east, with the Muckle (large) Cross visible through the trees.

58 On the left is a well-preserved townhouse built in 1694 which later became Braco's banking house. The Italianate building on the right was built in 1843 to house Elgin's excellent museum.

Appropriately sited next to the cathedral, the Biblical Garden is one of Elgin's more unusual **59** attractions. Biblical scenes are recreated and all 110 plants mentioned in the Bible are featured.

60 The remains of Elgin Cathedral, viewed from the west-end towers. Its many outstanding features include the country's finest octagonal chapter house, partly visible on the left.

Early morning light bathes the eastern elevation of Elgin Cathedral, **61** seen from across the River Lossie. The cathedral was established in 1224.

62 Independently run since 1797, Johnston's has been making beautiful knitwear, clothing and accessories from the most luxurious wools known to man for over two centuries.

Just north of Elgin is Spynie Palace, residence of the Bishops of Moray for five centuries. **63**
Inset: one of the corbels in the Great Hall, which supported the roof, now long gone.

64 Lossiemouth is Moray's main seaside town, established at the mouth of the River Lossie as a seaport for Elgin. Its harbour has become a marina for pleasure craft.

The buildings on Pitgaveny Quay were built as warehouses for goods going through the port **65** but now serve other purposes, such as housing the Fisheries & Community Museum.

66 Lossiemouth is an excellent base for coastal activities such as fishing, sailing,
wildlife watching or just enjoying the soft sandy beach and the dunes.

Glenfiddich Distillery (MWT), just outside Dufftown. It is little changed since 1886, **67** when William Grant and his nine children built the Distillery with their bare hands.

68 Dufftown was founded in 1817 by James Duff, 4th Earl of Fife, and is a typical planned town of the area with the main streets being laid out in the shape of a cross.

Balvenie Castle, Dufftown, was originally the seat of the powerful Comyn earls of Buchan. **69**
It is an enclosure castle with a massive curtain wall, now in the care of Historic Scotland.

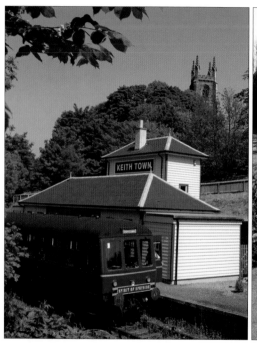

70 The market town of Keith straddles the Isla river.
Left: a Keith & Dufftown preserved railway train at Keith Town station. Right: Keith War Memorial.

Strathisla Distillery (MWT) goes way back to 1786, although it was not until the 1870s that this name was applied. Its annual capacity is 2.4 million litres.

72 Buckie was the largest town in the old county of Banff and is one of the largest in Moray. This is Cluny Square. Inset: the Speyside Way starts in the neighbouring community of Buckpool.

Buckie's Cluny Harbour was completed in 1880; lifeboats have been launched here for **73** over 145 years. The shipyard builds and repairs lifeboats like the one in the picture.

74 A few miles east of Buckie is Findochty, a particularly attractive coastal village.
    It is an ancient settlement, referred to as far back as the mid 10th century.

Findochty (pronounced Fin-ech-tay) harbour, in some ways like others 75
in the county, and yet offering a scene that is unique. See also p.80.

76 This aerial view of Portknockie, the next village east, shows that it is a well-planned village, laid out as neatly as the landscape allows.

The Bow Fiddle Rock is Portknockie's most visited attraction,
but the village as a whole deserves exploration.

78 The pleasing town of Cullen is last stop on this journey through Moray.
Here we look through the old railway arch up Seafield Street towards the town centre.

These rocky remnants frame Cullen beach as an explosion of cumulus cloud bubbles up over
the town. The coastline continues of course, but that takes us into the territory of another tour....

Published 2009 by Ness Publishing, 47 Academy Street, Elgin, Moray, IV30 1LR
Phone/fax 01343 549663 www.nesspublishing.co.uk
All photographs © Colin and Eithne Nutt except
p.15 © Ballindalloch Castle; pp.24/25 & p.76 © Scotavia Images; p.29 © Mark Williamson;
p.33 © Charlie Phillips; p.70 © Keith & Dufftown Railway
Text © Colin Nutt
ISBN 978-1-906549-05-3

Front cover: Telford's Bridge over the Spey at Craigellachie; p.1: Ballindalloch Castle gardens;
p.4: tower detail, St Giles' Church, Elgin; this page: a statue in Findochty;
back cover: spring on the Spey, Aberlour

For a list of websites and phone numbers please turn over >>>>

Websites and phone numbers (where available) in the order they appear in this book:

Moray: www.thisismoray.com
Speyside: www.greaterspeyside.com
Lossiemouth: www.lossiemouth.org
Cairngorms National Park Authority: www.cairngorms.co.uk
Sueno's Stone: www.historic-scotland.gov.uk (T) 01667460232
Tomintoul: www.visittomintoul.co.uk
Glenlivet Distillery: www.theglenlivet.com (T) 01340 821720
The Malt Whisky Trail: www.maltwhiskytrail.com (T) 01343 542666
Glen Livet Crown Estate: www.glenlivetestate.co.uk (T) 01479 870070
Grantown-on-Spey: www.grantownonline.co.uk
Revack Estate: Revack Lodge, Grantown-on-Spey, PH26 3NH (T) 01479 872234
Ballindalloch Castle: www.ballindallochcastle.co.uk (T) 01807 500205
Speyside Way: www.moray.gov.uk (T) 01340 881474
Cardhu Distillery: www.diageo.com (T) 01340 872555
Glenfarclas Distillery: www.glenfarclas.co.uk (T) 01807 500257
Ben Rinnes: www.speyside.moray.org/Aberlour/FoBR (T) 01340 871504
Archiestown: www.archiestown.com
Aberlour: www.speyside.moray.org/Aberlour
Speyside Cooperage: www.speysidecooperage.co.uk (T) 01340 871108
Rothes: www.speyside.moray.org/Rothes-on-Spey
Glen Grant Distillery: www.glengrant.com (T) 01340 832103
Baxters: www.baxters.com (T) 01343 820393
Fochabers: www.fochabers-heritage.org.uk
Whale & Dolphin Conservation Society: www.wdcs.org (T) 01343 820339